W9-CKR-170

50 One-Minute Tips for Retaining Employees

Building a Win-Win Environment

David K. Hayes, Ph.D. and
Jack D. Ninemeier, Ph.D.

A Fifty-Minute™ *Series Book*

This Fifty-Minute™ book is designed to be "read with a pencil." It is an excellent workbook for self-study as well as classroom learning. All material is copyright-protected and cannot be duplicated without permission from the publisher. *Therefore, be sure to order a copy for every training participant by contacting:*

Menlo Park, California

1-800-442-7477

CrispLearning.com

50 One-Minute Tips for Retaining Employees

Building a Win-Win Environment

David K. Hayes and Jack D. Ninemeier

CREDITS:
Senior Editor: **Debbie Woodbury**
Editor: **Luann Rouff**
Production Editor: **Jill Zayszly**
Production Manager: **Judy Petry**
Design: **Nicole Phillips**
Production Artist: **Zach Hooker**
Cartoonist: **Ralph Mapson**

© 2001 Crisp Publications, Inc.
Printed in the United States of America by Von Hoffmann Graphics, Inc.

CrispLearning.com

01 02 03 04   10 9 8 7 6 5 4 3 2 1

Library of Congress Catalog Card Number 2001090683
Hayes, David K. and Jack D. Ninemeier
50 One-Minute Tips for Retaining Employees
ISBN 1-56052-644-0

This book is printed on recyclable paper with soy ink.

Learning Objectives For:

50 ONE-MINUTE TIPS FOR RETAINING EMPLOYEES

The objectives for *50 One-Minute Tips for Retaining Employees* are listed below. They have been developed to guide you, the reader, to the core issues covered in this book.

THE OBJECTIVES OF THIS BOOK ARE:

❑ 1) To present tips for conducting new-employee orientation and training

❑ 2) To describe strategies for maintaining a professional workplace

❑ 3) To define ways to maintain positive employee relationships by using ongoing communication and maintaining a supportive and fun work environment

❑ 4) To outline the ways in which supervisors can help employees to help themselves become successful

❑ 5) To show managers and supervisors how their own feelings, attitudes, and experiences affect their employees and the workplace

ASSESSING YOUR PROGRESS

In addition to the learning objectives, Crisp Learning has developed an **assessment** that covers the fundamental information presented in this book. A 25-item, multiple-choice and true-false questionnaire allows the reader to evaluate his or her comprehension of the subject matter. To learn how to obtain a copy of this assessment, please call **1-800-442-7477** and ask to speak with a Customer Service Representative.

Assessments should not be used in any employee selection process.

About the Authors

David K. Hayes is the managing owner of a hotel in Lansing Michigan. He has over 25 years experience in directing employees at all levels of experience in the hospitality business. David is also the Editor of HospitalityLawyer.com, a website devoted to the legal, safety, and security information needs of the hospitality industry.

He received his Bachelor of Science (BS), Masters (MS) in Restaurant, Hotel, and Institutional Management, and a Ph.D. in Education from Purdue University. He is an accomplished author and trainer who has published popular university textbooks in the areas of hospitality business law, cost control, and employee training.

Jack D. Ninemeier is a professor at Michigan State University's School of Hospitality Business. He is the author, co-author, or editor of 28 books relating to the food-service and healthcare industries. He has also authored more than 175 trade journal articles.

He received his Ph.D. from the University of Wisconsin. He is a certified Hotel Administrator (CHA), Certified Food and Beverage Executive (CFBE), and Certified Hospitality Educator (CHE) as recognized by the American Hotel and Motel Association.

Dedication

This book is dedicated to employees in all types of businesses who are looking for confirmation that their employment decision was a good one, who desire to learn and to make contributions on the job, and who may want to become supervisors and managers someday.

It is also dedicated to employers and supervisors, who serve as links from where these employees are today to where they will go—in the organization specifically, and in the world of business more generally.

Lastly, this book is dedicated to Brother Herman Zaccarrelli, C.S.C., whose guidance and faith in the humanity of business managers everywhere and whose beliefs about the dignity of work have made this book a pleasure to produce.

Preface

This book presents tips for retaining employees, especially entry-level and/or hourly employees. These may include non-supervisory staff such as teenagers in their first job, retirees who are working part-time, and other non-technical personnel working at or near the organization's starting wage. Many of these tips apply to a wide range of businesses and many of the strategies will also work for professional and technical workers.

Managers and supervisors in all types of businesses understand the importance of retaining staff when the economy is strong and labor is short. Many of these same managers, however, fail to recognize that the retention of valuable staff is always desirable. Hiring and training are expensive, and valuable experience is lost with high staff turnover rates. Yes, it can be challenging to find and retain employees. Fortunately, you can use a variety of tactics to improve your retention rate.

Many employers believe that higher compensation is the only tactic for keeping employees from leaving. But "throwing money" at every operating problem is not the only solution. Clearly, employees must be paid at a competitive rate. However, compensation is more than an hourly rate or take-home pay. Benefits are also important, and while some of these are monetary, others are not. Many employees consider the friendliness and professionalism of the workplace, along with genuine respect from their employers, as incentives to remain on the job. These non-monetary attractions often influence whether a person stays or leaves.

The foundation for this book begins with you—your business culture and the philosophies and attitudes of management. A genuine interest in "internal marketing" (treating your employees the way you treat your customers) must precede the ideas outlined in this book, as only that can actually drive their implementation.

You are encouraged to complete numerous activities and exercises as you read this book. However, an underlying "assignment" is to objectively evaluate your business and workforce relative to the tips presented. Consider whether the tip will be useful just as it is presented. Must it be modified in some way to be most beneficial? Or, for reasons unique to the business, is it not applicable? Only you, with your detailed knowledge about your organization, can answer these questions. We hope you will discover many practical ideas in these pages to help you retain your employees and, in the process, help your business grow. It is for this purpose that the book was written, and against this purpose that its worth should be evaluated.

David K. Hayes

Jack D. Ninemeier

Contents

Follow Sound

Management Advice

Tip 1: Serve First and Lead Second

You probably landed your first job as a supervisor because you were good at what you were doing. If you successfully made the transition from employee to supervisor, someone had confidence in your abilities and in your potential to succeed. It is that same confidence and concern that your employees now seek from you.

Many supervisors truly believe that the purpose of a workforce is to make their boss look good. In reality, the best leaders spend the majority of their time helping to make those they lead look good. A manager is a servant first and a leader second, one who facilitates the work of employees in the following ways:

➤ By training them adequately

➤ By providing tools and equipment that are safe and well-maintained

➤ By removing obstacles to success

➤ By helping them resolve problems

➤ By providing them with continuing opportunities to learn on the job so they can prepare for promotions

Effective leaders serve their employees first so that everyone—both the employees and the supervisor—will be successful.

Gather Feedback

For a better perspective on how your employees view your management skills, ask them to answer the following questions. You may want to do this as part of an anonymous feedback gathering session or one-on-one with employees:

1. What could my supervisor start doing to help me perform better in my own job?

2. What should my supervisor *stop* doing to help me perform better in my own job?

ANALYZE YOUR LEADERSHIP SKILLS

Think about your own career and your best supervisors.

1. What are some qualities that make you think of them as the "best"?

   _____

   _____

2. Do you think you have some or all of these qualities?

   ❏ Yes   ❏ No

3. What things can you start to do right now and do every day so your own employees will consider you their "best" boss?

   _____

   _____

Now think about your own career and some of the supervisors you liked least.

1. Why do you consider them your least favorite supervisors?

   _____

   _____

2. Do you think you have some or all of these same faults?

   ❏ Yes   ❏ No

3. What are some things you can change right now so your own employees will not think of you as their least effective boss?

   _____

   _____

Tip 2: Establish Your Employee Average Retention Rate

After you have read this book and implemented the strategies you like, you will want to measure your success. To do this, you have to know where you began. The Retention Rate Worksheet can help you to do this. It is simple to complete and will tell you your average retention rate (ARR). It is hoped that you will see your ARR increase as you implement effective employee retention tactics.

Completing the worksheet

1. Enter each employee's name in Column (A), and then enter the total number of employees in Box 1.

2. Enter each employee's start date in Column (B).

3. Enter the current date in Column (C).

4. Calculate the total number of days that each employee has been with you. Enter that number in Column (D).

5. Add the number of days in Column (D), and enter this total in Box 2.

6. Divide the number of days in Box 2 by the number of employees in Box 1 to determine the average number of days that your entry-level staff has been employed for the current month.

7. Save this sheet to make it easier to compute next month's average.

6

Retention Rate Worksheet

Employee Name (A)	Employment Start Date (B)	Today's Date (C)	Number of Days Employed (D)
1.			
2.			
3.			
4.			
5.			

Total Number of Employees (Box 1)   Total Days (Box 2)

$$\frac{\text{Total Number of Days (Box 2)} \quad \boxed{}}{\text{Total Number of Employees (Box 1)} \quad \boxed{}} = \text{Average Retention Rate}$$

If you track your retention rate monthly, you can evaluate the success of the retention tactics you implement.

Tip 3: Estimate Your Turnover Costs

Some costs of turnover can be easily and directly calculated. For example, you can assess the cost of newspaper ads used to recruit new employees. The time you spend interviewing applicants, helping the new employee to complete necessary paperwork, and conducting an orientation session can be easily determined. However, many costs of turnover (and generally the most significant ones), cannot be calculated objectively; they must be estimated. For example, how could you accurately determine the following:

➤ The costs incurred by employees who know they are going to leave but stay on your payroll, and increasingly fail to meet standards of quality, quantity, customer expectation, and other standards

➤ The cost of providing a new employee with on-the-job training using a method in which both the employee and the trainer's time is sometimes spent in training for new tasks and sometimes spent in performing tasks that have already been learned

➤ The cost of the honest mistakes made by a new employee who wants to do well but who has yet to develop the knowledge and skills required for the job

➤ The cost incurred when your business is short-staffed and the available staff cannot meet quality standards

Calculating Turnover Costs

Employee turnover costs are estimated at between 50 to 100% (or more) of an employee's annual wage. Complete the exercise on the following page to obtain an estimate of your organization's turnover cost. The exercise illustrates three different turnover scenarios.

TURNOVER COST WORKSHEET

Average annual wage, including the cost of fringe benefits, you pay a full-time employee

$$\boxed{\$ \qquad}$$
Box A

Number of employees hired last year (nonseasonal) to maintain all full-time positions

$$\boxed{\$ \qquad}$$
Box B

Total wages/benefits paid for employees who left your organization

$$\boxed{\$ \qquad}$$
Box C
(Box A x Box B)

1. Assume the low estimate of turnover (50% of wages/benefits) is too high; for your organization, it is only 25% of the low estimate: Box C x 25%

$$\boxed{\$ \qquad}$$
Your Cost of Turnover

2. Assume the low estimate of turnover (50% of wages/benefits) is correct for your organization. Box C x 50%

$$\boxed{\$ \qquad}$$
Your Cost of Turnover

3. Assume the high estimate of turnover (100% of wages/benefits) is correct for your organization. Box C x 100%

$$\boxed{\$ \qquad}$$
Your Cost of Turnover

You will probably be surprised (if not astonished) at the annual cost of turnover for your entry-level staff. If you can implement no-cost or low-cost strategies to retrain your staff, they will clearly be cost-beneficial.

Tip 4: Follow All Applicable Federal and State Child Labor Laws

There are numerous laws related to teenage employees. All are important and, if followed carefully, help make your organization an employer of choice in the eyes of teenage employees and their families. Moreover, compliance with these laws will help you avoid potentially serious legal difficulties.

Federal Department of Labor regulations require that you keep records–including date of birth and occupation (position)–for all employees under the age of 19. You must also track their daily starting and quitting times and daily and weekly hours worked. You can protect yourself from unintentional violations of child labor provisions by filing an employment or age certificate for each youth you employ. Certificates issued under most state laws are acceptable for this purpose.

Familiarize yourself thoroughly with applicable child labor laws by contacting your state's Department of Labor. Make it clear to your employees that you and your organization are committed to following all applicable state and federal regulations.

Would you be willing to bet your business that you know *everything* you need to know about how federal labor standards apply to the employment of youth in your organization? Stiff financial penalties and negative public opinion stemming from violations can ruin a business.

Make sure you know *exactly* all of the following:

➤ Who is covered

➤ Restrictions on hours of work and/or occupations (e.g., what can covered youth do–and not do?)

➤ Penalties for violations of applicable provisions

➤ How the federal labor laws relate to state, local, and other federal laws

➤ Other aspects of the Fair Labor Standards Act that may apply to you

➤ Which, if any, of your jobs include tasks that are considered "hazardous" under federal law

➤ Where you can obtain further information

To learn about these and other requirements of employing youth under 19 years of age, visit the Federal Department of Labor's Web site: http://www:dol/asp/public/programs/handbook/childlbr.htm

Tip 5: Eliminate Workers Who Won't

Supervisors are sometimes accused of reducing hiring standards to that of "any applicant with a warm body." Of course, those who make these statements probably aren't supervisors who are often faced with days when only one of three workers has come in as scheduled (because one has called in sick and another has quit without notice).

Despite the temptation to hire workers immediately, however, you must not lower your selection or performance standards. The reason is clear: Your very best employees will not stay if you do!

Consider two employees. Tonya is a dedicated and solid worker who comes to work on time. Kyle often comes in late, works slowly when he does show up, and frequently calls in sick. When Tonya is scheduled to work with Kyle, she ends up doing far more than her fair share of the work. Would you be surprised if Tonya quit one day to go to work for a competitor who refused to allow employees like Kyle to take advantage of employees like Tonya? Retaining your very best workers is critical. To ensure that your best workers stay, eliminate those workers who cause them to leave.

Who Would You Assign?

	Good Employee	Poor Employee
1. To train a new employee	❏	❏
2. To do a special project	❏	❏
3. To provide a special service to one of your best customers	❏	❏
4. To work an extra-busy shift	❏	❏

You would assign the good employee in each case above, wouldn't you? As you do this, what incentive do you offer an employee to be "good"? (In other words, what do you give a "good" employee that you do not give to a "bad" employee?) The answer often is more work! Some supervisors, through their actions, actually provide a disincentive for an employee to do good work.

Don't take advantage of your good employees, even unconsciously. Using the following guidelines will help you keep your best workers:

➤ Ensure that all employees can work according to standards

➤ Eliminate employees who can't measure up to established standards

➤ Spread work assignments as fairly as possible

➤ Reward good employees for good performance

Tip 6: Eliminate Managers Who Can't

Tolerating poor performance from marginal *employees* will cause good employees to leave. Poor performance by *managers*, however, is likely to be an even greater cause of high turnover. You owe it to your employees to provide them with competent leaders.

You can easily identify your poor managers:

➤ They constantly need new employees to replace those who have quit

➤ They constantly criticize the quality of their workers

➤ They never have time to properly orient or train employees

➤ The accident rate of their employees is higher than those of other supervisors

➤ Customer complaints about the service levels of their employees are higher than those for other managers

➤ Standards relating to quality and quantity of work suggest substandard performance

➤ They are the source of continuous employee complaints

Poor managers cannot ask their employees to "go the extra mile" for the organization if the employees see that the manager will not "go the extra mile" for them. Poor managers seldom attain departmental productivity standards because the high turnover rates in their department prevents the establishment of an experienced staff that can meet (or exceed) required standards.

Many of these same managers and supervisors think that their work would be easier if they didn't have to deal with "problem" employees. In fact, however, the vast majority of all problems in an organization are caused by the supervisors and managers, not the employees. It is the supervisor—not the employee—who fails to adequately orient and train new employees, to coach and motivate them, and to provide an environment in which acceptable work can be done. Quality management is critical. To improve your retention rate, eliminate managers who can't manage to manage!

TAKE THE MANAGEMENT CHALLENGE!

How would an objective outsider rate you on each of the following management activities that directly relate to the performance of employees? Check (✔) one box for each responsibility.

How Well Do I Manage?	Inadequately	Very Effectively
1. Recruit the best possible applicants	❏	❏
2. Effectively orient new employees	❏	❏
3. Provide appropriate job training	❏	❏
4. Obtain employee feedback about problems that affect them	❏	❏
5. Provide ongoing coaching and performance appraisal	❏	❏
6. Provide required equipment and job tools	❏	❏
7. Implement ideas to help make the workplace professional and friendly	❏	❏
8. Properly manage change	❏	❏
9. Provide on-the-job opportunities to help employees meet personal goals	❏	❏

Tip 7: Manage Your Customers

Contrary to the old saying, the customer is *not* always right. That's right. Not only are customers sometimes wrong, where your entry-level workers are concerned, customers are sometime abusive, contemptuous, sexually inappropriate and/or verbally threatening. There's more bad news! You can be held legally liable for outrageous customer behavior (for example, if you knew, or should have known, about the behavior but did nothing to protect your employees). In addition, you can lose good workers if you sacrifice their goodwill in favor of the goodwill of an uncivilized customer.

This is not to say that customers are not vitally important. Of course they are. It is also important that all your employees be professional at all times. It is your job to ensure that they are. However, consider carefully how you should respond when your employees react to being abused by customers. Responses such as criticism and/or discipline, demands for an apology, and termination may, in fact, be very inappropriate. Not only do such responses fail to support your employees, they may open the door to potential lawsuits.

New employees are just learning about your expectations. They want to know that you will support them when they are right. They count on you to champion them. Don't sacrifice the integrity of your relationship with employees by tolerating intolerable customer behavior.

Determine Whether a Policy and Procedure Is Needed

How often do customers abuse your employees? Do you really know? Use the following steps to find out and to develop an action plan:

1. Discuss the topic at a regularly scheduled staff meeting or schedule a special meeting.

2. Ask the group for examples, if any, of customer abuse of any type.

3. If examples are given, lead a discussion that covers the following points:

    ➤ What specifically happened

    ➤ What, from the employee's perspective, led to the incident

    ➤ What, if anything, was done at the time and by whom

4. Provide the groundwork for the expected relationship between employees and customers. (The Ritz-Carlton Hotel chain's motto provides a good benchmark: Ladies and Gentlemen Serving Ladies and Gentlemen.)

5. Using the expectations defined in Step 4 as a foundation, discuss a basic procedure or process with your employees. Be sure to address the following:

    ➤ The extent to which inappropriate customer behavior is permitted. (This may need to be loosely defined as "when an individual employee begins to feel uncomfortable.")

    ➤ Establish that the next step is for the employee to summon his or her supervisor or the manager on duty. Agree on a dialogue such as, "Please excuse me while I get my supervisor." At this point, the supervisor can take over, using the conflict resolution skills in which she has been trained by her own boss.

When managing employees, remember that sometimes the customers are right and sometimes the employees are right. Have in place a procedure that can quickly and fairly assess the situation and define an appropriate corrective action.

16

Make First

Impressions Count

(Orientation)

Tip 8: Understand the Role of Starting Wages

Ask your new employees why they left one employer for another. How often do you hear, "I left for a better paying job"? Many experts argue about whether money motivates employees to remain at or move between jobs. Would most employees change jobs for 20 cents more an hour? For 20 dollars more a week? What amount would motivate you to change your current job? Significant amounts of money probably do motivate employees; small amounts of additional compensation may not.

Many employees can choose between different jobs in the same and in different industries. For example, a young person with good customer service skills can work in numerous fast-food outlets or in other retail businesses such as movie theaters, dry cleaners, tanning salons and grocery stores. Remember that you compete with many employers in different industries for your fair share of the labor force. Employees are likely to be attracted to your organization if you are known as an employer of choice within the community. Yes, compensation must be competitive (and competitive does not mean the highest in the community). However, when you follow sound management practices, conduct effective orientation and training, maintain a professional and friendly workplace, supervise the way you want to be supervised, and maintain ongoing communications, you are helping your employees to succeed. When job searchers can easily decide to choose your organization over the competitor's, you will know you have in place a very effective recruiting tool. Workers will come to your organization to enjoy a better job, not necessarily a better-paying job.

Managers who think, If we paid just 25 cents or 50 cents more an hour, our labor problems would be over, are probably kidding themselves. Substantially higher starting wages may yield a larger initial pool of employees, but your retention rate will not improve until you realize that neither you nor your employees work only for money.

Is Your Compensation Competitive?

1. What other businesses offering the same products and/or services as your organization compete with you for employees?

2. What other employers outside of your industry also compete for your labor pool of entry-level staff?

3. What is your entry-level starting pay, including fringe benefits?

4. What is the starting pay with benefits of other businesses that compete for your employees? (You can determine this in a number of ways: calling your "friendly competition," checking with fellow members of the chamber of commerce and other business associations, reviewing the classified ads in local newspapers, noting "help wanted" signs in store windows, and so on.)

5. Pretend an employee has informed you that he or she has been offered a similar position with a weekly pay that is 10% more than your wage rate. List some non-monetary benefits you offer that should make it worthwhile for your employee to remain with you. (Be sure to consider the retention tips discussed in this book, which address the problem of employees leaving for a nominal pay hike elsewhere.)

6. Non-monetary benefits we offer:

    _____

    _____

    _____

Tip 9: Inform Employees About Their Total Compensation

Do you pay entry-level workers as well as your competitors? Remember:

Wages + Benefits = Total Compensation

Some organizations try to lure your entry-level workers away with higher starting wages. These organizations, however, may offer fewer benefits. The starting wages (for example, hourly rate) of two competitors are easy to compare. Comparing the *benefits* offered by two employers, however, is much more difficult. Make sure your job applicants and present employees know the value of *all* benefits received from working in your organization. Communicate these to workers during their initial job interview and during their orientation program.

To succeed in the future, you need to create and deliver benefits that are important to entry-level workers—yet affordable for your company. If your organization has made a commitment to provide benefits, identify all of them and keep them visible.

For many employees, the lure of higher starting wages offered by a competitor can be real. Help your employees understand that their *total pay* is higher with you.

Determining Your Total Compensation Package

Use the following worksheet to calculate the total amount of compensation you pay to new and experienced employees and to part-time staff. Update the "numbers" as often as necessary and keep your employees current about the value of their benefits. (Note: If your organization has a human resources department, contact someone there to help with the calculations and to ensure that they are accurate.)

COMPENSATION WORKSHEET

Compensation/Benefit	Full-Time Employee (New Hire) (A)	Full-Time Employee (__ Months)(B)	Part-Time Employee (C)
Wage (hourly rate x hours worked per week)			
Employee Taxes			
FICA (Social Security)			
Compensation			
Other:			
Vacation Pay			
Insurance Benefits			
Health			
Dental			
Eyeglass			
Prescription Drug			
Other:			
Retirement Plan, 401(k) and/or other			
Other Benefits			
Tuition Assistance			
Uniforms			
Meals			
Personal/Sick Days			
Other:			
Total Weekly Compensation Package	$	$	$
	Box A	Box B	Box C

Note other benefits (employee discounts, estimated value of free/reduced employee services, and so on).

Tip 10: Explain the Long-Term Benefits of Staying

In most organizations, long-term workers qualify for benefits that recently hired workers do not. These may include automatic raises, subsidized tuition, extended vacations, and/or other forms of financial compensation and internal recognition.

Because these benefits are granted only to long-term employees, the advantages of qualifying for them may not be fully considered or understood by new employees. Don't let that happen! Keep long-term benefits highly visible to your entry-level workers. Review them in your new-employee orientation program and frequently during the initial employment period.

You know that your organization benefits when entry-level workers become long-term employees. Explain to your new hires how your organization repays that loyalty.

Consider Your Long-Term Benefits Package

Review the following benefits that are frequently available to employees who have stayed with an organization for at least 12 months. Check (✔) those that apply to your business. Keep a list of the benefits you offer highly visible to your employees.

- ❏ Medical insurance
- ❏ Dental/vision insurance
- ❏ Paid vacation
- ❏ Paid personal/sick days
- ❏ 401(k)/retirement plan
- ❏ Tuition assistance
- ❏ Family medical leave
- ❏ Other:

CALCULATE YOUR ADDITIONAL COMPENSATION

In Tip 9, you calculated the value of weekly compensation and benefits that accrue to full-time employees (new hires, Column A) and after required time on the job (Column B).

1. How much additional *weekly* compensation do "experienced" full-time employees receive in your organization?

Box B - Box A = Weekly Additional Compensation

2. How much additional *annual* compensation do "experienced" full-time employees receive in your organization?

Weekly Additional Compensation
x 52 weeks in year = **Annual Additional Compensation**

3. Be aware of opportunities you have to explain to your employees the long-term benefits of staying. Check (✓) any of the opportunities below that are available to you:

- ❏ During recruitment interview(s)

- ❏ During selection interview(s)

- ❏ During orientation sessions

- ❏ During career counseling sessions

- ❏ During conversations with mentor(s)

- ❏ In written job recruitment information

- ❏ In written job orientation information

- ❏ During performance appraisal sessions

- ❏ During ongoing staff meetings

- ❏ During ongoing coaching (one-on-one) sessions

- ❏ Other: _____

Tip 11: Share Your Vision

You have a vision of what you want your organization to be. Levels of service, revenue goals, and productivity standards are important to you. Make sure your employees know these goals and why they should be important to them. Imagine a train leaving a station. Every passenger knows the following:

➤ Where the train is going

➤ The purpose of his or her trip

➤ Why it is critical that the destination is reached

➤ What must be done to get there

Your employees want to know the same things about your organization. Whether your team is responsible for cleaning autos, serving a banquet, or renting videos, how you answer these questions is critical to creating an environment that encourages good workers to stay. The following exercise can help you define your vision and share it with your employees.

DEFINE YOUR VISION AND SHARE IT

List two important goals (visions) you have for your work group. For each goal, describe why it is important to your employees; and explain their role in attaining the goal.

Goal 1:

_____

_____

This goal is important to my employees because:

_____

_____

Here's what my staff can do to help reach our goal:

_____

_____

Goal 2:

_____

_____

This goal is important to my employees because:

_____

_____

Here's what our team can do to help reach our goal:

_____

_____

CONTINUED

CONTINUED

Now list some things that you can do to ensure that all employees know about your vision.

Ways to inform new employees about our vision:

_____

_____

Ongoing ways to inform and reinforce the vision to all employees:

_____

_____

Tip 12: Motivate Entry-Level Employees

When developing strategies and tactics to retain entry-level employees, you should recognize that there are two distinctions within this group. The first is new employees who hold entry-level positions for six months or less. The second is experienced employees who have been in an entry-level position for six months or longer.

You want to retain all entry-level workers that meet your team's productivity standards. However, the type of employee you typically employ helps determine the best retention strategies for you to use. For example, experienced employees may want to know how you can help them advance; new employees look to you to help them increase their comfort level and their sense of belonging on the team.

Be sure to choose the retention strategies that best meet the needs of your specific work team.

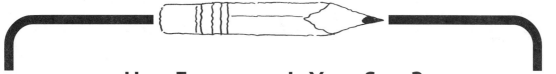

HOW EXPERIENCED IS YOUR STAFF?

You can determine what percentage of your employees are relatively new by dividing the total number of employees on the job for less than six months by the total number of entry-level employees:

$$\frac{\text{Number of new employees}}{\text{Total number of employees}} \quad = \quad \text{\% of new staff}$$

What are some tactics that can help retain your new employees?

_____

_____

What are some tactics that can help retain your experienced employees?

_____

_____

Tip 13: Conduct an Entrance Interview

In some organizations, managers seldom, if ever, meet one-on-one with an employee. New employees are usually impressed if, early in their employment, they can talk with upper-level management. Remember that new employees desire reinforcement for their decision to work for you. This early opportunity to show them that everyone in the organization cares about them can help establish an ongoing relationship, one that yields dedicated employees. The interview does not need to be long. Spend just a few minutes asking new employees about their families, their hobbies, and their aspirations for their new job. Get to know them as more than simply another "new hire." The more you know about your new employees, the better able you will be to match their needs with those of your organization. Employees appreciate a genuine attempt to understand them. Taking the time to hold entrance interviews improves your stature with your employees, builds morale, and increases your understanding of them. This knowledge can have a significant impact upon retention.

What Would You Like to Tell Your Boss?

Pretend you are a new employee. List some of the things you would like to tell your new boss (for example, what impresses you about the organization, what your career goals are, what you hope to learn on the job, and so on).

_____

_____

Do you think your new employees would like to tell you the same things about themselves?

❏ Yes   ❏ No

If yes, use the comments you just listed as guidelines for asking questions during entrance interviews.

Tip 14: Create Career Ladders

For many workers, the belief that an entry-level job can lead to more responsibility and better pay is very appealing. A *career ladder* is a road map that explains how advancement normally takes place. Of course, for some workers, entry-level jobs with your organization are intended to be only temporary. College students home for the summer, holiday workers, and those searching for permanent jobs in other fields are examples of employees who intend to remain for only a short period of time. However, some employees may be looking for a career; others may discover it with your help.

A career ladder plan is one way to show your employees how they can advance if they *do* stay with you. Take the time to analyze each entry-level position you offer. Consider how a talented individual holding that job could advance. Then create a career ladder that shows the progression in title, rank, and pay for that job. Review the career ladder with employees as part of your orientation, performance appraisal, and mentoring programs.

When entry-level workers look at your career ladder, they can envision a future for themselves as important, long-term employees.

HOW HIGH CAN EMPLOYEES CLIMB?

Consider the last entry-level employee you hired. If that employee stays with your organization and work performance is good, what position would he or she likely hold in the following four scenarios?

Rate of Pay

In one year: _____ $ _____

In two years: _____ $ _____

In three years: _____ $ _____

In five years: _____ $ _____

How do you currently help a new employee plan a future with your organization?

_____

_____

What other tactics could you use to get the word out about career opportunities with your organization?

_____

_____

Train! Train! Train! (and Do It Correctly)

Tip 15: Invest in Training

Imagine overhearing the following exchange at your next professional meeting:

Bernie: *"I can't afford to spend time and money training employees. It's all wasted if they leave."*

Latosha: *"That's true. But what if you don't train them and they stay?"*

Which of the two managers sounds most like you? Good managers know that training doesn't cost; it pays dividends. Yes, you might train an employee who leaves. But you don't know at the time of hiring which employee is going to stay. Training each new employee well sends a message to all employees that you care enough about them to train them—and that helps retention.

Yes, it can be challenging to consistently provide opportunities to those who are ready for them. You need to invest your own resources—both monetary and human—to develop and deliver the training needed to help employees meet your job standards. However, you may find other resources in your community that can help with your training responsibilities. For example, one organization reduces training costs by participating in chamber of commerce-sponsored sessions. Creative funding for training pays off for this organization, and it can pay off for yours as well.

INVESTIGATE YOUR TRAINING OPTIONS

Identify some local educational/training opportunities in your community that provide knowledge and/or skills development opportunities related to your organization. Use the following worksheet to determine which ones might be helpful to you.

Source of Assistance	Contact Person	Telephone Number	Type(s) of Training Provided
State and/or local employment commission			
High school vocational education programs			
Community/junior college programs			
Chamber of commerce			
Local/state professional associations			
Federally-funded welfare-to-work programs			
State rehabilitation services			
Other programs			

Don't know where to begin? Call your local chamber of commerce or your state/local employment service commission. Be sure to ask for referrals; for example, as you conclude your discussion with one source, ask them who else might be able to help you. This "nomination" system will yield lots of helpful information.

Tip 16: Encourage Employees to Try Your Product or Service

If you hire entry-level workers, you can strengthen your ties with them by having them sample the product or service they help provide. For example, the major auto manufacturers offer significant discounts to their employees. This helps create a connection between the workers, the products they produce, and the organization that employs them.

You may be able to do the same thing in your business. Consider reducing the cost of (or providing a complimentary sample of) the product or service you offer. For example, one hotel significantly reduced employee turnover after allowing newly hired housekeepers to spend a night in the hotel with their families at no cost. Restaurants often encourage wait staff to sample menu items. Retailers frequently offer employee discounts on merchandise.

If you want your employees to see the products they produce through the eyes of a consumer, give them a low-cost or no-cost way to become one. Your business will benefit when employees understand what makes your customers want your product or service. At the same time, you'll benefit from increased employee retention and the resulting lower turnover costs.

Don't Forget Follow-Up

After an employee has sampled your product or service, spend a few minutes obtaining some feedback. Some sample questions you can ask include the following:

- ❏ Did you like the product/service? Why or why not?

- ❏ Based on your experience, how would you describe the product or service to a customer who asked you about it?

- ❏ Would you recommend the product or service to a customer? Why or why not?

- ❏ Do you think our customers receive a value (price relative to quality) when they buy the product or service? Why or why not?

- ❏ What can we do to make the product or service better?

- ❏ Did your experience give you any ideas about other related products or services we could offer?

- ❏ Are you glad that you were able to sample the product or service? Why?

- ❏ Did sampling the product or service make you better able to produce (or sell) it? How?

- ❏ Do you think we should continue to allow employees to sample products or services? Why or why not?

Tip 17: Train Trainers to Train

When good employees are promoted to supervisory positions, some of their job tasks may stay the same, but they are now responsible for new activities, including scheduling, appraising the performance of, and training other employees. They don't just "magically" learn how to do these supervisory tasks.

Your organization may use a supervisor or an employee (or both!) to train new staff. Regardless of who does it and how it is done, the trainer must know how to train.

As stated earlier, the majority of all work-related problems are caused by the employer—not the employee. If you haven't trained your trainers, how can you expect them to know what to do? The first impressions of new employees are strongly influenced by how well (or how poorly) they are trained. You cannot delegate by "default" (in other words, by doing nothing). You must prepare the trainer.

What Do Trainers Have to Know?

Here is a checklist of some knowledge and skills that all trainers need to be effective:

❏ Knowledge about *exactly* how each job task is to be done

❏ The necessary tools and equipment to do the job correctly

❏ Knowledge of basic training principles

❏ A training plan (which indicates the *what*, *who*, and *when* of the training)

❏ Specific training lessons for each job task to be taught

❏ Adequate time to prepare, present, and follow up after the training

❏ Knowledge of follow-up coaching and counseling procedures

When you train your trainer(s) to train, everyone benefits:

➤ The trainers gain knowledge and skill, will be pleased that you trusted them to train, and will be motivated to do the best possible job

➤ The trainees receive higher-quality training

➤ Your customers will more likely receive products or services that meet their (and your) standards

➤ You and your organization will benefit from a new employee who is better prepared and who is gaining favorable first impressions about your organization

For more information on developing effective training, see the Additional Reading *list in the back of this book.*

Tip 18: Reward Your Trainers

How do *you* thank someone who has really helped you and your organization? Unfortunately, in the case of training, which is critical to your organization's success, the answer is often "I don't!" In fact, some supervisors in effect punish their trainers by requiring them to do all the necessary work they are normally assigned and, in addition, do training (see Tip 19).

All of us like some recognition from our managers when we perform a task well. So do your own employees. A sincere "thank you," along with a handshake and a genuine appreciation for a job well done is a good start at providing recognition. This kind of recognition can be exceptionally useful in an organizational culture that supports ongoing respect between employees and their supervisors.

Reward Ideas

Other ways to recognize your employee trainers (and others who train) include the following:

- ❏ Memos in their personnel files (which will be useful at the time of promotion consideration)

- ❏ Write-ups in your organization's newsletter, if applicable

- ❏ A social event for members of your "Trainer's Club" (such as attending a sporting event or enjoying a meal at a restaurant)

- ❏ Acknowledgement during your performance appraisal session(s) with the employee

- ❏ An invitation to attend an off-site training session conducted locally by an association, the chamber of commerce, or another group

- ❏ A personal subscription to a trade magazine

- ❏ Participation in supervisory meetings where training and related human resource topics are discussed

Tip 19: Relieve Trainers of Other Job Duties

Consider the following scenario: You need three sales clerks to work today. Because of your ongoing turnover problem, someone also needs to be trained. You schedule two experienced sales clerks and the trainee to work the same shift. If this sounds familiar to you, reconsider what is actually happening when you do this. You are really asking two people to do the work of three employees; and, in addition, you are asking one or both of the two longer-term employees to do additional work (train the new employee). With this all-too-common approach to training, everybody loses:

➤ The new employee does not receive proper training, begins to think the organization doesn't care, feels inadequate because he or she is unable to work to required standards, and feels stress because of the situation

➤ The experienced employees must work harder than is normally expected (because three people are usually scheduled for this shift), and they become resentful and begin to wonder if this is the job they really want

➤ The customers do not receive the product or service quality expected

If you use this approach consistently, you are likely to lose new employees, experienced employees, and customers; no one wins! Of course, there may be times when the preceding scenario cannot be avoided. In those instances, you need to acknowledge the less-than-ideal situation and your desire to avoid it in the future. You can accomplish that by keeping the following guidelines in mind:

➤ Allow trainees to learn and practice in an off-the-job environment or at a slow time when there are no or few customers

➤ Keep an adequate number of trained employees on the job at all times

➤ Keep to a minimum the number of tasks the experienced employee (trainer) must perform

➤ Train the trainer to train (see Tip 17)

Do You Ever Feel Overloaded?

1. How do you feel when your manager assigns you a special project (such as training someone) but does not provide you with adequate time to do it?

_____

_____

2. How do you feel if you think your boss "takes you for granted" and doesn't understand what your job really involves?

_____

_____

3. What suggestions could you make to your manager to help eliminate the problem? (How might these suggestions apply to you if they were made by your employees?)

_____

_____

Tip 20: Conduct Pre-Shift Training

Training is not needed only for new employees. All employees need ongoing training. They must learn about new products and services; about procedures that address problems you, your customers, or your staff are facing; and about many other issues that arise in our fast-paced world. This training must be well thought out before being presented. It does not, however, have to be expensive or extensive.

Many organizations routinely use pre-shift training sessions to help their employees "keep up" with desired or necessary changes.

There is some evidence that pre-shift training can be very successful. The Ritz-Carlton Hotel chain (the only hotel company in the world to win the coveted Malcolm Baldridge National Quality Award) conducts pre-shift training for all employees on every shift at every hotel in the world. In fact, every employee is taught some general information according to a pre-planned schedule.

Pre-shift training can eliminate surprises. If a product is unavailable or in limited quantity, if there is a sale, if conditions have changed since the last work shift, and so on, your employees will know. This can eliminate embarrassment. Additionally, it is another step in your ongoing effort to show your employees that you care about them, that they are "part of the solution" (not the problem), and that everyone is an important member of the organization's team.

Sample Agenda for a Pre-Shift Meeting

1. Special announcements (daily specials, production schedules, company policy announcements, and so on)

2. Carryover from yesterday's meeting (issues discussed at previous meeting that you couldn't fully cover)

3. Questions and answers

4. Employee suggestions

5. A "work tip" of the day (which might be offered by you or an employee)

6. A special word of praise and thanks, which reflects your respect and gratitude for your employees

Maintain a Professional Workplace

46

Tip 21: Strictly Enforce a Zero-Tolerance Harassment Policy

Title VII of the federal Civil Rights Act prohibits sexual and other forms of harassment in the workplace. The penalties for violating these laws are the same as those for other types of civil rights violations. To guard against liability from harassment charges, and to ensure a quality workplace for all employees, you should allow zero (no) tolerance of objectionable behavior. Harassment in any form can cause good people to leave your organization. Professional supervisors and managers make it clear to all workers that harassment will not be tolerated.

No employee should need to tolerate harassment and the stress and anxiety it creates. No organization needs to divert time, money, and other resources away from business purposes to address the turnover, lawsuits, and other problems on-the-job harassment creates. Enforcing a zero-tolerance harassment policy is good for your employees and your organization.

Most organizations today include their harassment policy in their employee manuals. Other companies have gone further by posting the policy in common areas such as lunchrooms and on bulletin boards. The policy should be discussed at new-employee orientation sessions and at other ongoing staff meetings.

An effective harassment policy should include the following:

- ➤ A statement that the organization unequivocally supports a zero-tolerance standard

- ➤ A definition of the terms and behaviors discussed in the statement

- ➤ A clear description of acceptable and unacceptable behaviors

- ➤ An explanation of the reasons for the existing policy

- ➤ A discussion of the consequences of unacceptable behavior

- ➤ Specific procedures to be followed after a complaint is lodged

- ➤ Several avenues for bringing a complaint or concern(s) to the attention of management

- ➤ Identification, by name, of the employer representative to whom complaints should be reported

- ➤ A clear statement that all complaints and investigations will be treated in confidence

How Are You Combating Harassment?

Use the following checklist to ensure that you have implemented and are maintaining a zero-tolerance harassment policy.

	Yes	No	Actions Needed	Deadline
Our zero-tolerance harassment policy is written and included in our employee handbook.				
Our harassment policy is reviewed during our new-employee orientation session(s).				
Our harassment policy is reviewed with current employees on a regularly scheduled basis.				
Our harassment policy is posted in employee common areas.				
Employees have a choice of at least two individuals to whom they can report an incident of harassment.				
Allegations of harassment are promptly investigated and handled in accordance with our organization's policy.				

Tip 22: Create a Culturally Diverse Workforce

Demographers estimate that by the year 2040, there will be no majority workers in the United States. Everyone, regardless of ethnic background, will be a minority. That means you will have a minority workforce, even if you don't have one now.

Recognizing a diverse workforce is important because employees tend to remain in a comfortable environment; they will leave an environment in which they are uncomfortable. It is important to maintain, at all levels of your organization, a workforce that reflects the makeup of the community in which you operate and attract your workers. These employees bring unique and necessary ideas to your workplace. They also help make new entry-level employees feel "at home," and they can provide the on-the-job support and hospitality that encourages new employees to stay with you.

If you want to increase the number of potentially excellent employees you hire, remember that diversity is not about counting heads, but about making heads count. Only you can set the tone in your workplace. Embrace the efforts necessary to create an environment that reflects diversity as well as your commitment to providing opportunities to *all* your employees.

How are you supporting cultural diversity?

How would you honestly rate your organization's efforts to recruit a culturally diverse workforce?

Superior   Average   Fair   Poor

How would you honestly rate your own personal efforts to support diversity in the workplace you manage?

Superior   Average   Fair   Poor

What are some specific ways in which a culturally diverse staff can help your organization?

_____

_____

Your department?

_____

_____

Your employees?

_____

_____

Yourself?

_____

_____

Describe a personal employment experience in which a culturally diverse workforce improved the professionalism and/or comfort level of your organization.

_____

_____

How can you be more supportive of efforts to increase the cultural diversity of your department or organization?

_____

_____

Tip 23: Make Employee Safety a Top Priority

Attention to worker safety is directly related to your employee retention rate. When an employee is injured at work, this presents a cost to your organization in terms of workers' compensation claims—and possibly in terms of higher insurance rates. Injured employees may not be able to or want to return to work. Effective employee retention programs guarantee *many* important things, and emphasizing employee safety goes a long way toward implementing your professional and personal concerns for the welfare of your employees. In the process, you create an atmosphere in which your staff is confident of your concerns for them.

A safe facility is a combination of two factors:

➤ A well-maintained environment (physical plant, store, office, and so on)

➤ Effective operating policies and procedures

If workers perceive their jobs as unsafe, they will find another. By demonstrating a real commitment to worker safety, you show your employees that you care about them. This commitment is important to all employees, regardless of their age or experience.

EXAMINE YOUR COMMITMENT TO SAFETY

To obtain one measure of the emphasis your organization places on employee safety, answer the following questions:

Yes No

- ❏ ❏ Is safety training an important part of your employee orientation process?

- ❏ ❏ Are employees tested on their safety knowledge after critical safety training is completed?

- ❏ ❏ Do employee files contain a record of the safety training successfully completed by each staff member?

- ❏ ❏ Is safety training ongoing?

    Date of last safety discussion at a staff meeting: _____

    Date safety was last discussed at a pre-shift meeting: _____

- ❏ ❏ Does the organization (or your department) have an active Employee Safety Committee that meets at least monthly?

What do your answers say about your commitment to safety? What *exactly* will you do to address any questions to which you answered no?

_____

_____

Tip 24: Ensure Reasonable Accommodations for Disabled Employees

The Americans with Disabilities Act (ADA) prohibits discrimination against people with disabilities in the area of employment. Complying with the ADA simply makes good business sense. For those workers who are disabled, what counts is not what they lack, but what they do with what they have. Studies have shown that disabled employees are as dependable as or even more dependable than other workers are. These employees may need extra help to get started, but they will be among your most reliable.

The ADA does not require you to hire an unqualified disabled applicant. You can still select the most qualified candidate if no applicant was eliminated from consideration because of a disability.

You must make what is termed "reasonable accommodation" for your disabled workers. You will have provided reasonable accommodation when you do two things: make existing facilities readily accessible to individuals with mobility impairments or other disabilities, and restructure jobs in the most accommodating manner possible to allow disabled individuals to perform them.

Reasonable accommodation does not require an undue hardship for your organization. Accommodations could be as simple as providing a ramp for wheelchair access, lowering shelves, increasing light levels, or providing large-print job aids or other print-based materials, depending on the employee's limitation.

WHAT IS "REASONABLE ACCOMMODATION?"

Consider the following "reasonable accommodation" issues each time you are considering filling a job with a disabled individual:

1. Can the applicant perform the essential functions of the job with or without reasonable accommodation? (It is legal to ask this question.)

   ❑ If no, the applicant is not qualified and is therefore not protected by the ADA.

   ❑ If yes, go on to question 2.

2. Is the necessary accommodation reasonable? (To answer this question, ask yourself the following: Can this accommodation be made without creating an undue financial or administrative hardship on the business?)

   ❑ No. (Remember that you are not required to provide unreasonable accommodations.)

   ❑ If yes, then go on to question 3.

3. Will this accommodation or the hiring of the person with the disability create a direct threat to the health or safety of other employees or customers in the workplace?

   ❑ If yes, you are not required to make the accommodation, and have fulfilled your obligation under the ADA.

   ❑ If no, the individual should be given equal consideration for the vacant position.

For more information about hiring employees with disabilities, see The Americans with Disabilities Act, *by Mary B. Disckson, Crisp Publications, 1995.*

Tip 25: Share Financial Numbers with Employees

Most employees like to feel that they are "in the loop" regarding what is going on in their department or organization. They want to feel that their boss respects and trusts them enough to share information that wouldn't be provided to others, including customers and the general public.

Some organizations post monthly financial information for all employees to see. Some even conduct paid training, or briefing, sessions to teach employees what the numbers mean and how they might be interpreted. Sharing financial information does not need to be "all or nothing." If you (or your boss) do not think a total financial picture of the organization can be revealed, you might want to provide some other statistics such as:

➤ Daily and month-to-date revenues

➤ The number of units produced or the number of orders shipped (or average value of unit shipped)

➤ Customer feedback information

➤ The number of customers served

Select data upon which employees can have a direct impact. Show them that they are an essential part of the team, and genuinely solicit their feedback about what the numbers mean.

Some organizations conduct contests to "beat" the numbers. For example, you might set a sales goal and challenge all employees to beat it. This is a much better tactic than one in which one employee must win and others must lose. A "beat the number" contest can be win-win for all employees.

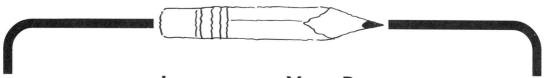

IMPLEMENTING YOUR PLAN

1. Would you like it if your boss shared more financial information with you?

   ❏ Yes   ❏ No

2. Do you think your employees would like it if you shared more financial information with them?

   ❏ Yes   ❏ No

3. What financial or other information not currently being shared with employees can you begin to share?

   _____

   _____

4. Where can you post this information? (Select a place that is convenient to all employees.)

   _____

   _____

5. When can you explain to your employees what you are doing and why? (Consider a pre-shift meeting or placing it on the agenda of your ongoing staff meetings.)

   _____

   _____

6. What might be the rules and prizes for a contest in which employees work to surpass existing financial targets?

   _____

   _____

Supervise As You Would Like to Be Supervised

Tip 26: Enforce "On-Time" Policies Fairly and Consistently

Employees do not like it when supervisors favor one worker over another. This can cause resentment, with some employees feeling that they have no real future with the organization because they are not part of the "right" group of staff members. Employees watch your actions carefully.

This retention tip requires consistency. Never allow some employees to arrive at work later than their scheduled time with no consequences while other tardy employees are subjected to punishment. Not only does this type of inconsistency put you on questionable legal grounds, you will also be seen as a manager who shows favoritism—a trait your employees will justly feel is unprofessional.

Your "on-time" policies should address employees arriving for work and returning from meal periods and scheduled rest breaks. Policies should be fair and reasonable. Getting input from your employees as you prepare these policies can be helpful. The policy (like all others you use) should be properly communicated and uniformly enforced. It is the consistent enforcement of your standards that will mark your managerial style as firm but fair.

Review Your "On-Time" Policy

	Yes	No
Your on-time policy has some tolerance for tardiness when:		
arriving at work	❏	❏
returning from rest breaks	❏	❏
returning from meal breaks	❏	❏
Your on-time policy is:		
discussed during new-employee orientation sessions	❏	❏
presented in your employee handbook	❏	❏
reviewed during ongoing staff meetings	❏	❏
Your on-time policy was developed with input from employees	❏	❏
Your on-time policy is fairly and consistently enforced with all employees	❏	❏

Tip 27: Be Careful Not to Over-Schedule

Your employees may not be able to work as often as you want them to. If you schedule your staff for more hours than they desire, you may cause some of your employees to quit. Others may stay, but be frustrated because they think you are taking advantage of them. Stress also results when employees must set a priority on their job, their family, and their other interests. Remember that retirees may be limited in the number of hours that they can work while retaining full social security benefits. Seasonal workers on public assistance may also face limits on their earnings in order to keep their benefits. Teenagers may be limited in their work hours by law, their parents, and/or by school schedules. Despite your desire to properly staff your business in the short run, don't over-schedule. The long-term solution to staffing problems is to retain your current employees. Over-scheduling is a surefire way to increase—not reduce—turnover.

Consider Your Employees' Work Preferences

Feel free to copy the form on the following page. Ask employees to complete it when they are first hired, and to update it whenever their preferences change.

To: All Employees

Subject: Your Preferred Work Schedule

We know that you are very busy and have important personal commitments. Please help us know when you are available for work by completing the following work schedule. Then let's make a deal: We'll try to schedule you at your preferred times, and you do your best to keep these schedule commitments.

Please write in the times when you are *normally* available to work:

Name	Sun	Mon	Tues	Wed	Thur	Fri	Sat

If your preferred times change, please submit another "Preferred Work Schedule" form. Thank you.

Tip 28: Give Employees a Personal Copy of Their Work Schedule

Sometimes, posting one general schedule for all employees isn't sufficient to guarantee you are adequately staffed. Consider the following three cases:

➤ Akeem is a great employee–when he makes it to work on time on the correct day. Like many active teenagers, he is constantly switching his schedule around to accommodate his busy social life.

➤ Mara is also a great employee. She was referred to her company from a community agency that specializes in helping mentally challenged persons become work-ready.

➤ Mario, a third employee, cannot read; in his current position, language fluency is not necessary.

Each of these examples illustrates a case in which a supervisor can make a special effort to work with employees to ensure that they are aware of their work shifts or schedules for the next several days. Posting a schedule on the employee bulletin board is an effective communication strategy for most–but certainly not all–employees. Supervisors can help these otherwise good employees become excellent staff members who meet all expectations, including complying with work schedules.

Employee Schedule Form

The following schedule form can be reproduced, completed, and personally handed to applicable employees. Taking a moment to review the schedule can help provide the necessary reinforcement, as can "reminding" the employee at the end of every shift when he or she is next expected to report to work. (Note: To avoid embarrassment, provide and discuss the schedule privately.)

Work Schedule For

_____

(Employee Name)

Day/Date	Work Time	
	Begin	**End**
Monday		
Tuesday		
Wednesday		
Thursday		
Friday		
Saturday		
Sunday		

Tip 29: Seek Out Employee Assistance Programs

Some employees need extra help in making the transition to full- or even part-time work. When they obtain this assistance, it can greatly increase their ability to be successful. If they work for you, it can improve your retention rate.

Welfare-to-work, on-the-job training programs, job placement services, and subsidized work programs exist in many cities. To find them, check with your state employment agency, local schools, and your chamber of commerce. Ask these officials what, if any, services they offer and whom else they advise you to contact. Then let the people in charge of those programs know about the employment opportunities your organization offers.

Some of your employees may require help after they are on the job and have been performing successfully. Sometimes employees encounter personal problems (including alcohol or other substance abuse, financial difficulties, marital problems, and other types of off-the-job challenges) that can affect their attendance, their ability to consistently meet required standards, and their personal interactions with you and other employees. Although it is not your job to solve any of these personal problems, you can show your concern by directing them to places where they can receive proper professional assistance.

Don't assume that the people in charge of these assistance programs won't be interested in your organization. They appreciate employers who take an active interest in the success of their workforce. When they find such an employer, partnerships can develop, and these partnerships can work for you. To get started, use the following log, adapting it if necessary to your own organization's needs.

ASSISTANCE PROGRAM CONTACT LOG

Use the following log to record specifics of your search for employee assistance programs. Save it; in the future, you will know who–and who not–to contact.

Date _____   Name _____

                                                 Agency _____

Call in Future   ❏ yes ❏ no   Phone _____

Notes _____

_____

_____

Date _____   Name _____

                                                 Agency _____

Call in Future   ❏ yes ❏ no   Phone _____

Notes _____

_____

_____

Date _____   Name _____

                                                 Agency _____

Call in Future   ❏ yes ❏ no   Phone _____

Notes _____

_____

_____

Tip 30: Invite "Fast-Track" Employees to Attend Management Meetings

Employees who feel valued and who believe that you or someone in your company has important plans for them in the future are more likely to stay with you than those who do not feel valued or recognized in any way.

How can you make employees feel good about themselves and increase their interest in remaining with your organization? One way is to include them in the things that are going on in the workplace.

Employees often wonder what their bosses do "behind the closed doors." Some are convinced that their supervisor's meetings relate to employees and how to further exploit them! Consider inviting appropriate employees (or even most or all employees on a rotational basis) to attend all or some of your management meetings. They will get a big picture of the organization—its challenges, its operating strategies, and its future—and they may have helpful suggestions.

Using this strategy can help employees feel like part of the team, and it will provide further evidence of the genuine respect for and interest in open communication between supervisors, managers, and employees.

Getting Started

1. From your perspective, what are the advantages and disadvantages of allowing an employee to attend a management meeting?

   _____

   _____

2. What might the advantages and disadvantages be from an employee's perspective?

   _____

   _____

3. How might you determine which employee(s) to invite?

   _____

   _____

4. What types of issues could be discussed when an employee was present?

   _____

   _____

5. What types of issues, if any, should not be discussed in the presence of an employee?

   _____

   _____

6. What must you do to implement this strategy?

   _____

   _____

7. Set a date when this strategy will be in place.

   _____

   _____

Tip 31: Implement a "Catch the Employee Doing Something Right" Program

Many supervisors pay more attention to minor infractions than to positive experiences with their employees. For example, Pedro may have come to work on time and in the proper uniform every day for the last three weeks without his supervisor acknowledging this. Then, on the first day of the fourth week, Pedro arrives late and is scolded.

Several customers have also commented to the supervisor about the great work Pedro does, but the supervisor does not pass on this praise to Pedro. However, when another customer has a minor problem involving Pedro, the supervisor "lets him have it."

The supervisor is a coach who should thank and praise employees, encouraging them when they do something right. If you are not in the habit of praising your employees, or don't think that it is something you could easily do, consider initiating a simple plan that will get you started:

Guidelines for a "Catch the Employee Doing Something Right" Program:

➤ Recognize that praising employees and offering encouragement can be an important strategy in your employee retention efforts.

➤ Use a staff meeting to tell employees about the recognition program.

➤ Make copies of the "I Caught You Doing Something Right" coupons below.

➤ Give copies of the coupons to other managers and supervisors, to employees, and, if applicable, to your customers.

➤ When an employee is caught "doing something right" give him or her a coupon, which can be accumulated until the end of the month.

➤ The coupons can be turned in and tallied, and winners announced. (For example, any employee receiving a specified number of coupons is entitled to a prize-dinner for two, a gift certificate, favored parking, or another applicable gift.)

Supervisors who look for and find what is positive about their employees are likely to enjoy positive results; supervisors who emphasize the negative are likely to see negative consequences.

I Caught You Doing Something Right!

Employee Name _____

Date _____

Time _____

Comment (what happened) _____

_____

Observer _____

Thanks!

Tip 32: Conduct an Exit Interview with Employees Who Leave

To increase retention, you must know why your employees leave. Conduct an exit interview (in person if possible, or by telephone if necessary) with each employee you lose. The reasons given for leaving can help you plan future retention strategies, so make it easy for them to be candid with you. Interview employees who leave involuntarily as well as voluntarily.

Keep a record of the reasons for leaving and analyze them to see if patterns emerge in areas that you can control. For example, exit interviews that consistently indicate workers are leaving because the work is too hard may really be saying that more training is needed, or even that workloads should be reduced. If a large number of employees from one particular department quit because their supervisor is "mean and unfair," that may suggest the supervisor needs training in human relations skills. These are problems you can influence. By contrast, a teenager who leaves because his or her parents are moving out of state is not something you can control.

Remember: You can use the information you get from departing workers to avoid losing future employees.

SAMPLE EXIT INTERVIEW FORM

Name of employee: _____

Interview date: _____

1. On a scale of 1 to 5 how would you rate this job?

1	2	3	4	5
Bad	Below Average	Average	Above Average	Great

2. What did you like most about the job?

_____

_____

3. What did you like least about the job?

_____

_____

4. Why are you leaving our organization?

_____

_____

5. Would you recommend this job to a friend?

❏ Yes   ❏ No

6. How could we make the job better?

_____

_____

7. Do you have any other comments/suggestions?

_____

Encourage Ongoing Communication

Tip 33: Hold Employee-Focused Meetings for Non-Management

Are employees included in your regularly scheduled staff meetings? These sessions can be critically important to improve communication between non-management workers and their supervisors and managers.

Plan to hold staff meetings that include non-management employees at least twice monthly. Some supervisors do all the talking at their staff meeting—and then the meeting is over! Don't let that happen at your meetings. Tell your employees what they need to know, then give them a chance to talk to you about their concerns. It is a good idea to distribute an agenda in advance so employees have time to consider what they might want to contribute to the discussions. Remember that the primary purpose of these meetings is improving communication and identifying concerns that you can address.

PLAN YOUR STAFF MEETINGS

1. Who should attend?

   _____

   _____

2. What is the best day?

   _____

   _____

3. When is the best time?

   _____

   _____

4. Where should the meeting be held?

   _____

   _____

5. How long should the meeting last?

   _____

   _____

6. Who will facilitate the meeting?

   _____

   _____

CONTINUED

CONTINUED

7. When will we hold the first meeting?

_____

_____

8. What topics should be discussed?

_____

_____

9. How will employees be told about the meeting?

_____

_____

10. How can I include any employee(s) who will not be scheduled for work at the time of the meeting?

_____

_____

11. How can I encourage employees to identify special concerns at the meeting?

_____

_____

Tip 34: Communicate the Benefits of Your Unique Organization

How would you complete the following sentence?

"One good thing about working at (your organization) is…

_____

_____

How you complete the preceding sentence can make a big difference in your employee retention rate. Every organization has characteristics that make it special and enjoyable for its employees. Sometimes the benefits include discounts on products and services sold by the organization. In other organizations, benefits might include extensive customer contact, outdoor work, a quiet and comfortable office setting, or the knowledge that the work is of great importance. Any organization can emphasize the welfare of employees and provide an enjoyable work culture.

Highlight the features of your organization that can help attract and retain workers seeking those benefits. These advantages help make your place of employment unique and enticing to potential employees. Don't forget to highlight what you personally like about your organization. By analyzing your own reasons for staying, you give your employees some.

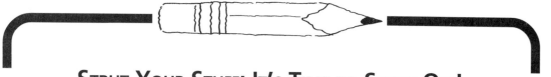

STRUT YOUR STUFF: IT'S TIME TO SHOW OFF!

Nearly all organizations offer attractive benefits to their employees. Use the following space to list some benefits people will enjoy when they work for your organization.

Benefit One:

_____

_____

Benefit Two:

_____

_____

Benefit Three:

_____

_____

Benefit Four:

_____

_____

Benefit Five:

_____

_____

Tip 35: Create an Employee Retention Council

When managers focus their attention on a specific aspect of their organization, it generally experiences noticeable improvement. Retention is no exception, and one way you can emphasize it is to develop an Employee Retention Council.

This is a group that meets regularly to discuss ways to improve employee retention. The council can consist of fellow managers and supervisors within your organization, business associates with similar concerns, experts and advisors such as high school counselors and college faculty, and even your own boss. Members of your local community service and/or trade association(s) likely share your concerns and might become involved in the council.

A retention council can help you by providing a forum to learn about the best retention practices of others and to share your own. If you are not aware of an existing council, seek your supervisor's approval and then start one. Be active in it. Not only will you be able to practice your leadership skills, you will be doing your employees and your own organization a tremendous service.

Who Wants to Be a Member?

In the space provided, list the organizations or individuals you will contact to help develop an Employee Retention Council:

Name	Telephone Number	Email address
1. _____	_____	_____
2. _____	_____	_____
3. _____	_____	_____
4. _____	_____	_____

Tip 36: Recognize Employee Birthdays

Do you view your birthday as a special day or just another day? Even if you don't personally make a big deal out of it, perhaps your friends and family do. It is interesting that some organizations treat their customers in special ways on their birthday (for example, restaurants often provide a free meal). However, these same organizations often fail to recognize the birthdays of their own employees.

Implementing the tips in this book helps develop a "family" of co-workers. This family can recognize the birthdays of its members by providing a birthday card (whether it is mailed or presented in person), by having a birthday party, and/or by showing some other form of recognition.

Give birthday recognition a try. It might sound corny to you, but it often has real meaning to your employees.

Getting Started

1. Would my employees like having their birthday recognized? (If in doubt, ask some of them!)

   ❏ Yes   ❏ No

2. What are some simple things I can do to recognize employee birthdays?

   _____

   _____

3. When will I implement my birthday recognition strategy?

   _____

   _____

Tip 37: Make Daily "Howdy" Rounds

Don't be a manager who only talks to your employees to make assignments or to discipline them for mistakes. Make daily "howdy" rounds to:

➤ Talk briefly with each employee about issues not specific to the job (for example, family or current events). If you don't know your employees' interests, this will get you acquainted with them.

➤ Ask employees for specific suggestions about how you can better assist with job-related activities. For example, ask if all necessary tools/ equipment are available, if work schedules are appropriate, if procedures for requesting time off are adequate, and so on.

➤ Ask about what you are doing that *hinders* the employee from more effective work performance. You can also inquire about organizational policies and procedures that impede effective output. After suggestions are made, take corrective action as soon as possible.

Create a Friendly Workplace

Tip 38: Use Employee Recognition Programs

When employee recognition programs are used, staff members are publicly or privately praised for a specific reason. There may or may not be a monetary reward given as part of the recognition.

For many employees, verbal recognition for a job well done is as effective a motivator as is a cash reward often associated with incentive programs. Recognition letters from you, announcements on employee bulletin boards, plaques, and special recognition pins are all ways you can let your employees know that you recognize their accomplishments and value their work.

Include your employees' ideas when developing your recognition programs. When possible, include employee input when selecting award recipients. Criteria for recognition programs might include:

➤ Cleanest work area

➤ Fewest absences

➤ Best safety record

➤ Best new idea

➤ On-time record

➤ Completion of special project(s)

➤ Customer Service

➤ Meeting or exceeding goals or standards

Create programs that work best for your own employees, but remember to repeat programs often, enabling different employees to be recognized. In addition, when possible, use award factors that do not favor a few staff members. (For example, a program with "votes" from retail customers wouldn't impact warehouse workers.)

Getting Started

If you do not already have a recognition program in place, use the following worksheet to get started.

List types of recognition awards you could use to publicly or privately recognize employees:

Criteria	Frequency	Recognition or Reward

Tip 39: Build a Great Team and Praise It Often

The best attract the best. Everyone wants to associate with a winner. That is why colleges and universities with a winning team in a popular sport such as football or basketball usually enjoy increases in new student applications and financial contributions. Your employees want to be the "cream of the crop": the best at what they do.

If you allow continued poor performance by an employee, you communicate to the best of your staff that it is okay if the team is not as good as it can be.

You should help poorly performing employees, because your commitment to coaching and training is critical to having a winning team. If you want to retain your star players, make sure all new employees know they have joined a successful team; and then treat them like the professionals they will become. The best of your staff want to associate with others like themselves. You can do a lot to help them become successful.

What's in a Name?

1. List some positive terms that you and others in your organization could use to describe your winning team. Examples include efficient, dedicated, professional, creative, goal-oriented, and so on.

   _____

   _____

2. What are some examples of daily opportunities for you to praise your team using these descriptions?

   ❏ When an exceptional deadline has been met

   ❏ During project status meetings

   ❏ When introducing an employee to someone from outside the organization

   ❏ Other:

   _____

   _____

Tip 40: Write a Personal Letter to Parents of Teenage Employees

Parents want to be proud of their children. A letter from you to the parent(s) of your teenage employees can be beneficial to both you and your young employees. First, it helps to assure the parent(s) that their son or daughter is working for a reputable, professional, and concerned employer who has the best interests of the teenager at heart. Second, it helps develop an unofficial alliance between you and the parent(s), who can help provide guidance when work-related issues arise, such as not showing up for assigned shifts, working only partial shifts, or seeking other employment.

A PARENTAL LETTER CHECKLIST

When writing your letter to parents of employees, consider incorporating the following points:

❑ Your appreciation that their teenager has joined your business team

❑ A pledge to provide the young employee with the proper orientation and training needed to help achieve success on the job

❑ Your interest in providing the youthful employee with additional training, which will identify and help prepare the teenager for career opportunities with your organization and/or industry and beyond

❑ An interesting, job-related anecdote in which the teenager performed effectively and achieved an early success

❑ An offer to serve as a mentor to help the young worker with any job-related questions or issues

❑ Your willingness to talk with the parent(s) at any time about the young worker's job-related performance or any other matters affecting employment

Tip 40 was contributed by David Berger, a restauranteur in Lansing Michigan. To contribute your own tips to this publication, please see p. 108.

Tip 41: Share Scheduling Responsibilities with Employees

Work shift schedules can be a major problem for many employees. This is especially true for teens with school functions, social engagements, and family-related activities that often take priority over work commitments. Supervisors often fail to help negotiate this balance, which causes difficulty in creating a work schedule seen as fair by both parties.

The solution is simple: Allow employees to participate in the scheduling process. For example, assume each of your part-time employees is needed to work five shifts (four hours each) weekly. Assume also that you have 10 employees. Therefore, 50 shifts must be scheduled. Involve workers in the scheduling process by allowing them to request to work (or not to work) specific time slots in a way viewed as "fair" by your entire work team. Ask employees to help you build the "fair" scheduling system. They will welcome the opportunity.

By involving employees in the scheduling process, you increase their commitment to the schedule and to your organization. Both of these tactics have a positive effect on your retention rate.

Rules for the Shift Bidding Game

Use a bidding process to identify employee "no-work" preferences for *applicable* shifts (for example, employees in school during the day clearly cannot work midday shifts during the week; no-work preferences for these shifts would not be relevant for these workers). Other rules might include the following:

➤ Each employee, in turn, can mark a shift that he or she does not want to work on the first round of bidding

➤ Employees repeat the process on the second round of bidding

➤ You then complete the schedule, recognizing employee no-work preferences as you do

➤ When conflicts arise, discuss the issue with the affected employees, keeping in mind who may have compromised the last time

A spirit of compromise within a company culture of fairness and respect for employee desires can help to reduce scheduling conflicts, which affect retention rates.

Tip 42: Reward Employees Who Work on Non-Scheduled Days

Does the following scenario sound familiar? Faruq is an excellent employee: great attitude, super performance, and a dedication to the job you rarely see in employees. In fact, he is the one person you can count on to come in on his scheduled days off to fill a shift when someone calls in sick or quits without notice. One day, Faruq tells you he has found a new job. He shakes your hand, offering no reason for leaving.

Why did this happen? Simple. Instead of rewarding Faruq for his dedication, his supervisor failed to recognize how his life (and all employees have one!) was continuously disrupted.

When employees must work on scheduled days off, treat them special. Recognition, rewards, and extra benefits are among the ways to thank these workers. If you take care of your dedicated employees by rewarding them when they come in on scheduled days off, you will keep your best!

Don't always request the same employee to work an extra shift, just because he always says yes or because someone else always says no. Even with rewards, overworked employees will begin to feel that they are being taken advantage of.

WHAT CAN YOU DO?

Identify three tangible rewards you can give to an employee who works a non-scheduled shift:

1. _____

2. _____

3. _____

How and when will you inform your employees about the problem of covering previously scheduled shifts, and your new strategy of compensating employees who work them?

How: _____

_____

When: _____

_____

Tip 43: Invite Family Members of New Employees to Visit Your Workplace

Whether a new employee is young, older, or retired, he or she may have family members who are interested in the employee's new position. Invite parents of teens to visit and learn firsthand what their child does. This enables you to show the hospitable environment you offer; it can also help build parental support. For older or married workers, invite spouses or significant others, as well as family members, to visit. Let them know how pleased you are to have the new employee in your organization. Some employers even extend this invitation to potential employees and their families before final hiring decisions are made.

All employees want to be proud of what they do, and their families' opinion of their work and workplace is very important. Using this no-cost or low-cost morale booster can be a meaningful part of your employee retention efforts.

How Would You Improve the Sample Letter?

The letter on the next page is double-spaced so that you can revise it as you would write it. After completing your own version, arrange to have it delivered to family members of your new employees. You are likely to be surprised at the important role this tactic can play in establishing a long-term relationship between you and your staff members.

SAMPLE INVITATION LETTER

Here is a sample letter that you might revise, as necessary, and put on your organization's letterhead:

Dear _____,

Just a brief note to tell you how happy we are that *(employee's name)*

has begun working with us. I would like to personally invite you

and/or other family members and friends to visit us to learn more

about what we do and how *(employee's name)* helps us.

I am looking forward to meeting you and to working with your

(specify relation; for example, son, mother, aunt, and so on).

Please feel free to call me at 123-4567 if you would like to arrange

a time to visit.

Sincerely,
(Your Name)

Tip 44: Make the Workplace Fun

Someone once defined work as "any activity that isn't fun." It doesn't have to be that way, and it shouldn't be. For today's employees of all ages, fun at work can be a tremendous attraction. Of course, the tasks for which your team is responsible must be completed; however, having some fun at work *is* both possible and desirable.

Simply ask your employees what you can do now to make your workplace more enjoyable. What a great way to find out what motivates them! They may have great ideas that *do not* negatively affect productivity, and *do* positively affect their attitudes. Implement the best ideas. Also, talk to fellow managers and learn what activities they use to spark enjoyment in their workplace.

Work in any organization need not be boring. If it is, then it is your job to change it. If you don't, you'll lose your employees to those managers with the courage and imagination to recognize that it takes a lot more than money to keep employees around.

Making Your Workplace Fun

Use the space below to record your ideas for making your organization a fun place to work.

Current Activities

* _____

* _____

* _____

Possible Activities

* _____

* _____

* _____

Help Your

Employees

Succeed

Tip 45: Identify State-Approved (Licensed) Childcare Options

A lack of consistently dependable or high-quality childcare is a frequent reason for employee absences and worry and stress on the job. Some employees will have access to friends, family members, or other dependable sources of childcare. Unfortunately, other employees will not. "Good" employees must also be "good" parents; what would you do if faced with the choice of going to work as scheduled or providing care for your children? As an employer, you can help your employees avoid this dilemma, which creates a win-win situation for everyone and helps to ensure that a good employee will stay on the job.

Keeping a Childcare Checklist

Contact the branch of your state's children's agency (the name will vary by state). Obtain a list of all licensed/registered childcare providers in your area. Help all employees who may need these services to identify childcare providers located near them.

A CHILDCARE ASSISTANCE CHECKLIST

Date: _____

State agency that licenses childcare providers: _____

Contact Person: _____

Telephone number: _____

Checklist:

❑ Our list of licensed childcare providers is less than six months old

❑ Our list is included with orientation information for applicable employees

❑ Employees are assisted in finding an on-demand childcare facility for use when regular childcare is unavailable

❑ Brochures/information from providers who have been successfully used by current/past employees are available and provided to interested employees

Note: Inquire about discounts that may be available when your employees use a facility for a specified number of care days monthly.

Tip 46: Reward Success in Each Employee

When employees are asked why they quit a job, the answer is often, "No one cared about me or the work I was doing." Satisfaction at work is a powerful motivator. Unfortunately, in some entry-level jobs, the work is routine and repetitive and it may not be possible to restructure a job otherwise. In nearly all entry-level jobs, however, you can help create a motivating environment.

Almost every employee can demonstrate success in some area, and these strengths provide the key to the recognition you can give employees. If you have a worker with excellent attendance, make sure that he or she knows you appreciate this dedication. If another worker is especially good at customer service, compliment him or her on that trait. Your attention to employee success will pay off with improved employee self-esteem and retention. Make sure that none of your employees can ever say that they left your company because "No one cared about the work I was doing."

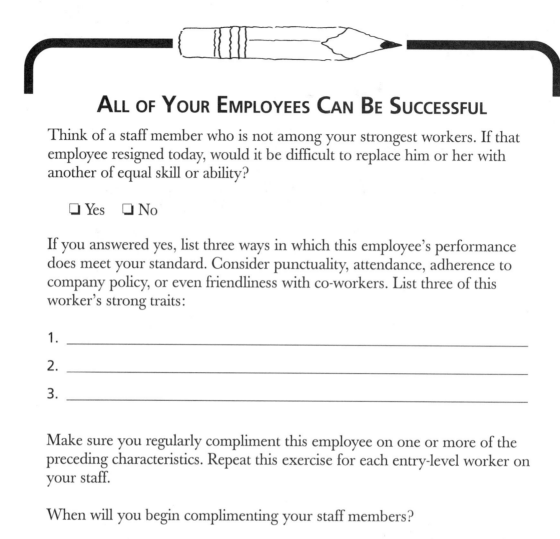

ALL OF YOUR EMPLOYEES CAN BE SUCCESSFUL

Think of a staff member who is not among your strongest workers. If that employee resigned today, would it be difficult to replace him or her with another of equal skill or ability?

❏ Yes   ❏ No

If you answered yes, list three ways in which this employee's performance does meet your standard. Consider punctuality, attendance, adherence to company policy, or even friendliness with co-workers. List three of this worker's strong traits:

1. _____

2. _____

3. _____

Make sure you regularly compliment this employee on one or more of the preceding characteristics. Repeat this exercise for each entry-level worker on your staff.

When will you begin complimenting your staff members?

_____

_____

Tip 47: Recognize Your Employees' Eldercare Responsibilities

Many employees must care for elderly relatives. The parents of the baby boom generation are living longer than any generation before them. It is estimated that between 15% and 25% of all U.S. households contain elderly parents or friends for whom eldercare must be provided. Therefore, it is increasingly likely that part of your workforce must care for elderly relatives. These circumstances create special needs that you should recognize and address.

Employees who are responsible for elderly relatives need flexible work schedules that enable them to provide adequate care. You can assist them by accommodating their schedules whenever possible and by identifying programs and organizations in your area that can provide help. Just as childcare programs are important to some of your younger employees, so are eldercare programs important for older workers. Help employees with eldercare responsibilities to balance their family obligations with the demands of their jobs; you'll improve your retention rate in the process.

Getting Started

1. How can you determine which employees have eldercare responsibilities?

_____

_____

2. What local agencies are available that may be able to provide information, resources and/or other services for the elderly?

Agency Name	Contact Person	Telephone Number

(Be sure to provide this information to applicable employees.)

Tip 48: Don't Punish Your Best for Being Good

If you give your best employees more work than you give to mediocre employees, you may be falling into a trap that can have severe negative effects on your retention rate. Many supervisors tend to give extra work—such as training a new employee or undertaking a special project—to their best employees. They know that these special employees will do the work without complaint and do it well. This tactic probably makes sense to us, but it can be viewed as a punishment by your best employees, who may think something like the following:

"Why should I do my job as quickly as I can if I'll just have to pick up the extra work of those who are slower?"

"Why should I do my work a lot better than others if this will just make the boss give me extra work assignments?"

"Why should I work extra hours to cover for an employee who is always late or absent?"

Why be a superior employee if the company's only rewards for such behavior is extra work? Your best employees should be given some recognition and reward for both the routine and the special work they do for you. You can provide that reward and improve your retention rate when you don't punish your best employees for being good. Find tangible ways to reward their extra efforts.

Reward; Don't Punish

List three non-monetary organizational rewards you can grant to employees who regularly excel at their jobs.

1. _____

_____

2. _____

_____

3. _____

_____

Tip 49: Go to Lunch

Regardless of how busy you are, there is always a daily opportunity to learn more about your employees and the work environment you have created: lunch. You can arrange to take your employees out to lunch or sit with them in a common eating area. (If your work schedules don't permit this, you might be able to arrange a breakfast or dinner.) Periodically, arrange to dine with one or more of your employees.

Your goal for sharing a meal is simple. In a relaxed and informal setting, find out what is going right for and what is troubling your best and brightest employees. Then you can address any issues they raise.

Use meal experiences as a listening opportunity. Use at least two-thirds of the time you spend with the employee(s) listening and learning about their opinions. You can't fix their problems until you understand them fully. Listening—not talking—is the best way to determine which corrective actions, if any, are necessary.

Fortunately, most of the issues that employees generally raise *will* be within your control to remedy. Remember that factors *within the manager's control* are the most frequently cited reasons why employees leave a job. Make sure you know what those factors are so you can remove those obstacles to your employees' success.

Tip 50: Help Employees Learn About Public Transportation Systems

Some employees may have a hard time getting to work for various reasons. Some may not have cars (or reliable ones). Available parking for your business may be distant and/or expensive. Maps or charts illustrating public transportation routes may be less than friendly to read, understand, and interpret (this may be especially true for employees for whom English is a second language).

Some employees may want or need to use public transportation occasionally; others may be required to use it all of the time. This includes employees with physical or mental challenges and those with no other alternative. A little legwork (no pun intended) on your part can make it easier for your staff members to learn about the availability of public transportation to help them travel to your workplace.

Here are some suggestions:

➤ Determine the closest bus, train, subway or other public transportation stop/station to your work location.

➤ Record the names and telephone numbers of the most reliable taxicab companies. (You may be able to negotiate a discount for your employees, and even customers, if the service is used frequently enough.)

➤ Include a directory of any information you find in your new employee orientation material.

➤ For employees who need public transportation, provide the appropriate maps, and indicate the site of the nearest stop or station to the employee's home. If necessary, you can also trace the route to work and/or provide written or oral directions.

➤ In addition to route maps, affected employees will also need a time schedule for the method of public transportation used.

TRANSPORTATION RESOURCE LIST

Public Transportation System(s)	Telephone Number	Location of stop closest to business	Transportation System Map Available
			❏ Yes ❏ No
			❏ Yes ❏ No
			❏ Yes ❏ No
			❏ Yes ❏ No

WANTED: YOUR RETENTION IDEAS

We hope you'll share your creative ideas about how to retain employees. If you modify or improve upon a strategy or tip in this book, or create new tips that might be shared with fellow supervisors and managers, we would like to hear about your suggestions.

Feel free to use and copy this form, and send or fax it to us.

Tip:

_____

_____

_____

Implementation suggestions:

_____

_____

_____

Your name and address:

_____

_____

_____

If we use your idea in another book, we will cite you as the contributor and send you a complimentary copy.

Please send to:

Jack Ninemeier
Broad Graduate School of Management
Michigan State University
239 Epply Center
East Lansing, Michigan, 48824-1124
Fax: 517-432-1170.
Email:ninemeie@msu.edu

Additional Reading

Berry, Janice and Barb Wingfield. *Retaining Your Employees*. Menlo Park, CA: Crisp Publications, 2001.

Dell, Twyla. *Motivating at Work*. Menlo Park, CA: Crisp Publications, 1993.

Dickson, Mary B. *The Americans With Disabilities Act*. Menlo Park, CA: Crisp Publications, 1995.

Doucet, Betsey and Juliana Lightle. *Sexual Harassment in the Workplace*. Menlo Park, CA: Crisp Publications, 1992.

Hathaway, Patti. *Giving and Receiving Feedback*. Menlo Park, CA: Crisp Publications, 1998.

Hart, Lois B. *Training Methods That Work*. Menlo Park, CA: Crisp Publications, 1991.

Hayes, David K. and Jack D. Ninemeier. *50 One-Minute Tips for Recruiting Employees*. Menlo Park, CA: Crisp Publications, 2001.

Hayes, David K. and Herman Zaccarelli. *Training Managers to Train*. Menlo Park, CA: Crisp Publications, 1996.

Haynes, Marion E. *Effective Meeting Skills*. Menlo Park, CA: Crisp Publications, 1997.

Hunt, Jim and Claire Raines. *The Xers and the Boomers*. Menlo Park, CA: Crisp Publications, 2000.

McArdle, Geri. *Delivering Effective Training Sessions*. Menlo Park, CA: Crisp Publications, 1994.

McDowell, Joyce. *Promoting Safety*. Menlo Park, CA: Crisp Publications, 2000.

Minor, Marianne. *Coaching and Counseling*, Third Edition. Menlo Park, CA: Crisp Publications, 2002.

Raines, Claire. *Beyond Generation X*. Menlo Park, CA: Crisp Publications, 1997.

Simons, George and Amy J. Zuckerman. *Working Together*. Menlo Park, CA: Crisp Publications, 1994.

Wingfield, Barb and Janice Berry. *Retaining Your Employees*. Menlo Park, CA: Crisp Publications, 2001.

NOTES

Now Available From

CRISP. Learning™

Books • Videos • CD-ROMs • Computer-Based Training Products

Subject Areas Include:

Management
Human Resources
Communication Skills
Personal Development
Marketing/Sales
Organizational Development
Customer Service/Quality
Computer Skills
Small Business and Entrepreneurship
Adult Literacy and Learning
Life Planning and Retirement

50 One-Minute Tips for Retaining Employees

VERK

CRISP WORLDWIDE DISTRIBUTION

English language books are distributed worldwide. Major international distributors include:

ASIA/PACIFIC

Australia/New Zealand: In Learning, PO Box 1051, Springwood QLD, Brisbane, Australia 4127   Tel: 61-7-3-841-2286, Facsimile: 61-7-3-841-2618
ATTN: Messrs. Gordon

Philippines: National Book Store, Inc., Quad Alpha Centrum Bldg, 125 Pioneer Street, Mandaluyong, Metro Manila, Philippines   Tel: 632-631-8051, Facsimile: 632-631-5016

Singapore, Malaysia, Brunei, Indonesia: Times Book Shops. Direct sales HQ: STP Distributors, Pasir Panjang Distrientre, Block 1 #03-01A, Pasir Panjang Rd. Singapore 118480   Tel: 65-2767626, Facsimile: 65-2767119

Japan: Phoenix Associates Co., Ltd., Mizuho Bldng, 3-F, 2-12-2, Kami Osaki, Shinagawa-Ku, Tokyo 141   Tel: 81-33-443-7231, Facsimile: 81-33-443-7640
ATTN: Mr. Peter Owans

CANADA

Crisp Learning Canada, 60 Briarwood Avenue, Mississauga, ON L5G 3N6 Canada
Tel: 905-274-5678, Facsimile: 905-278-2801
ATTN: Mr. Steve Connolly

Trade Book Stores: Raincoast Books, 8680 Cambie Street,
Vancouver, BC V6P 6M9 Canada
Tel: 604-323-7100, Facsimile: 604-323-2600   ATTN: Order Desk

EUROPEAN UNION

England: Flex Training, Ltd., 9-15 Hitchin Street,
Baldock, Hertfordshire, SG7 6A, England
Tel: 44-1-46-289-6000, Facsimile: 44-1-46-289-2417   ATTN: Mr. David Willetts

INDIA

Multi-Media HRD, Pvt., Ltd., National House,
Tulloch Road, Appolo Bunder, Bombay, India 400-039
Tel: 91-22-204-2281, Facsimile: 91-22-283-6478   ATTN: Messrs. Aggarwal

SOUTH AMERICA

Mexico: Grupo Editorial Iberoamerica, Nebraska 199, Col. Napoles, 03810 Mexico, D.F.
Tel: 525-523-0994, Facsimile: 525-543-1173   ATTN: Señor Nicholas Grepe

SOUTH AFRICA

Alternative Books, PO Box 1345, Ferndale 2160, South Africa
Tel: 27-11-792-7730, Facsimile: 27-11-792-7787   ATTN: Mr. Vernon de Haas